>>UNLEASH LEARNING

>> 40 SUCCESSFUL STRATEGIES TO IGNITE, INSPIRE AND UNLEASH LEARNING FOR EVERYONE

DR WILLIAM DEJEAN

US Edition

Email   william@ williamdejean.com
Web   www.williamdejean.com
Facebook   www.facebook.com/drwilliamdejean
Twitter   twitter.com/william_dejean
ABN   65 609 232 847

Editor   Camille Howard
Design   Madeleine Preston
Production   ARMEDIA

ISBN 978-0-9808242-0-9

"This very useful volume speaks clearly to both the heart and the practical strategies of his vision of in-depth connectedness with learning. It will be an asset equally for beginner teachers and trainers, and for critically assessing and refreshing experienced teaching."

Dr Robyn Moloney,
senior lecturer, School of Education, Macquarie University

"His strategies helped our teachers to develop more powerful classroom conversations through dedicated planning to seek each student's voice."

Michele C. Staves, M.Ed
assistant principal, Tredyffrin-Easttown School District

"Rather than accepting compliance and conformity this book reminds us that being a teacher involves innovation and creativity in order to enable real learning."

Dr Louise Hard,
associate dean (courses) Charles Sturt University

"I have witnessed firsthand many of the strategies included in this book. As such, I can genuinely say, both from my personal experience and the positive feedback received from participants, they really do unleash learning for everyone!"

Lorraine Madden,
trainer, facilitator, mentor, coach

"*Unleash Learning* reminds me about the moral commitments to equity and quality that should inform the work of all educators ... This book shows how leaders can balance accountability with high quality teaching and learning."

Elaine Hazim,
campus principal, Victoria University Secondary College

"Congratulations William on creating a gift for all educators ... You have infused this book with 'pearls of wisdom' many of which highlight the psychology underpinning teaching and learning."

Dr Suzy Green,
clinical & coaching psychologist, founder, The Positivity Institute

"His strategies helped me to believe that I can make a difference, it directed my way of thinking and his stories became the benchmark tools that I continue to explore to inspire everyone that I teach."

Peter Klein,
'creative music teacher' Belvoir Special School

"Not only will *Unleash Learning* strengthen your personal teaching, but it will strengthen our profession as well."

Professor Jeff Sapp,
College of Education, California State University

acknowledgements

I wish to thank the thousands of students I have had the privilege of working with over the past 20 years. You helped me see what worked and what didn't. You invited me into your life's celebrations, and let me know when the journey hit difficult times. Throughout it all you reminded me that learning, when unleashed, can transform, inspire and awaken us all. I might have been your teacher but you taught me as well.

Thank you to my partner Robert for telling me, "It's now time to write your book!" and for continuing to encourage me each step of the way.

To my parents for providing inspiration, generous assistance and consistent messages of love and kindness. You continue to be an example. Thank you.

I wish to acknowledge the team at ARMEDIA for your work in bringing this book to visual life. Thank you for your professionalism and creativity.

To Elaine and Lorraine for reading early drafts of this book and providing important feedback and insightful suggestions. Thank you for your time, professionalism and support.

And finally to Marcia, for telling me if I wrote it you would read it. And you did, so many times. Thank you for the Skype calls, editing sessions and wonderful advice. There are insufficient words to truly express my gratitude. But I will continue to try...

To educators everywhere,
whose work makes things better for our world.

INTRODUCTION

PART I: PREPARE

PART II: UNLEASH LEARNING
HOW TO START

WHAT TO DO IN THE MIDDLE

HOW TO END

PART III: REFLECT

≫INTRODUCTION

WHO THIS BOOK IS FOR

>> If you are a teacher, university educator, staff developer, trainer, presenter or speaker, this book is for you. This book is for you because you are passionate about what you know, you are inspired by what you want to share, and you sometimes find it difficult to ensure the passion, wisdom and knowledge you care so deeply about translates into deep learning for your audience. It is for you, because the world needs your gifts, knowledge, talent, insight, passion, enthusiasm and understanding, and any way to unleash that will benefit us all.

This book is designed to give you additional tools and resources to unleash the best of what you do, and ensure the learning is unleashed for your students, participants or audience members. This book is for you, because you don't want your learners remembering your inspiring, exciting and life-changing information, knowledge or experiences for a short period time; rather you want the work you do to be transformative, life changing and something they will keep forever—why provide a gift if it is opened and then put on a shelf? Learning can be a box that once opened, changes everything. This book is written to help you find additional ways to help your learners open up that box.

My story

I have been a high school teacher, university teacher in the United States and Australia, classroom coach, staff developer and consultant for a major educational non-profit, TEDx presenter, and I have been leading professional development sessions and retreats for innovative organizations in various fields. I have been living and breathing teaching and learning and developing innovative ways to unleash learning for nearly 20 years.

Today I am passionate about inspiring and re-inspiring innovative organizations for the important work they do. Whether you are in social inclusion, education, mental health, wellness, leadership or other change-making professions, you are a teacher. Your work is designed to show us what is possible, to help us get better or to learn something new. I work to ensure those people who are working to make a difference (that's you!) have the tools, wellness, focus and inspiration needed to successfully do their important work. I hope this book does this for you.

That "story" in your head

When I worked with new teachers at the university level, I often saw the biggest blockage for their success was in their head. By that I mean that in our head is the collective consciousness of the "story" of what it means to teach and learn. The problem for us as educators (whether you are a presenter, staff developer, trainer or educator of any kind) is that not only do we have a story in our heads about what it means to teach and learn, we also have a very specific story in our heads about what teachers are "supposed" to do and what students are "supposed" to do. The story in our head has been created by many factors, including the following facts:

▶ We have been to school.

▶ We have family members who have been to school and share their school stories.

▶ We have watched movies or TV shows about teachers and teaching (and most times, they are pretty bad).

▶ We are constantly surrounded by images in magazines, billboards or other advertising that depicts this story of what it means to be a teacher.

Let's look at the story in your head. Is there a chalkboard? What is the teacher wearing? Is the teacher standing in front of students? Are chairs in rows and the teacher is talking. How are the students supposed to be behaving? What is the teacher supposed to be doing? What does the classroom look like?

What if you are a university educator or lecturer? Do you see a large theater where the teacher is standing with quiet students watching? Or are there a few students engaged, raising their hands and answering a few questions the educator asks. Where are the students sitting in the lecture theater? How are they supposed to be behaving? How are you supposed to be acting?

What if you are a speaker or staff developer? I'm guessing this story of speaking and teaching is in your head too. What does the staff developer do and what should his or her learners do? How is the room arranged? Who does most of the talking?

Perhaps you don't have those images in your head, or it isn't the story you recall when you think about teaching and learning. You might think that, but the minute you stand in front of a group of learners, you might find you revert to one of these stories. It's like we turn into a character in a play that has been written so deeply into our being that it is hard not to play it out. You play this role and I play that role. I will be the teacher and you will be the student. I dress like this, you behave like this. Even the most innovative people I have worked with seem to slip into a role the moment they stand in front of a group of young people, present to an audience or become an educator at a university.

Yet, to unleash the best learning for the people you are working with, the first thing you need to do is to have the courage to disrupt this story in your head, and replace it with a new story. We will get to that new story shortly.

Banking models of education— there is another way

Paulo Friere is one of my heroes. If you haven't read his books, you might consider getting your hands on them (of course, after you are done with this book— we still have work to do!). Friere introduced me to many important ideas, including the banking model of education. The model is like the story we have all experienced and, for the many educators I've worked with, it's part of the story they have in their heads. It's the story that makes up so much of our experience of learning,

or of those movies we have seen about school. Just like depositing money in the bank, this educational model is all about filling empty heads with information. In this model, the all-knowing-teacher bestows information (like a fact factory) to the empty vessels that are the students. When the focus of the instruction is facts, facts, facts, which students must learn, learn, learn, you know you are in a banking model of education.

Now don't get me wrong, sometimes we need to do all the talking, read the PowerPoint slides, ask questions to a few students, set the classroom up in rows, or convey some very key important information. But if you are reading this book, you are interested in creating the kind of learning that will stick with your students, that will be transformative, and that will cause them to remember your presentation, class or staff development session for a long time.

So to unleash learning for everyone (yes, everyone!) I'm going to ask you to interrupt that story and replace it with a new story, one that is found in the gym.

You know you are in a banking model of education when:

- someone is reading his or her bullet points on PowerPoint to you
- the teacher lectures for the entire hour, with no responses from the "passive" students
- the teacher asks a question, a few people answer it and the teacher lets the students know if it is right or wrong
- you are doing all the talking in the class
- you are asked how you "deliver" your lesson or presentation
- the classroom is in neat rows
- the system tells you to "just put your teaching online"
- the students are trying to guess the answer the teacher wants.

The new story: lifting the weights

A personal trainer has one goal: to get you healthy. When you work with a personal trainer, they focus on ensuring you are working out for the entire session. For example, a personal trainer knows that for muscle to be built, you must **lift the weights** during the entire session. The muscle does not get built from the trainer talking, explaining or demonstrating. The potential of your muscle is unleashed in the moments you are **lifting the weights**. And you can't just lift the weights a few times. You have to lift the weights over and over again. As the muscle fires, you get stronger and stronger.

The same is true in learning, although the "muscles" we are most interested in are the muscles of the mind, heart and spirit. These are the locations where learning is unleashed, and transformation, deep learning and memory is stored. Each time you create opportunities when your learners' muscles "fire", you are creating the moments when learning is being unleashed for them. So every time you create intentional, planned, ongoing, structured, mindful opportunities for learners to:

▶ speak it

▶ teach it

▶ explain it to others

▶ draw it

▶ sing it

▶ repeat it

▶ summarize it

▶ write it

▶ read it to someone

▶ dance it

▶ discuss it

▶ question it

▶ engage with it

▶ discuss it with others

…you are getting them to **lift the weights.**

And just like a personal trainer, you can't get your students to lift the weights a few times. You have to get them to lift the weights over and over again. The real art is creating the strategic, mindful, thought through, intentional opportunities when *all* of your learners are **lifting the weights.**

This book is designed to help you do that.

Who you are matters

You have a powerful, important history that brings you to the work you do. You come from a rich background of experiences, thoughts, frameworks, opinions, pains, joys, sorrows, and a powerful life history. Whether you believe me or not, you see your work and your pedagogy through the lenses of your life, history, identities and experiences. You see the world in very unique ways.

While a banking model of education sees learning as "objective facts" that must be "learned", I'm here to remind you that to truly unleash learning for *everyone*, who you are matters.

For example, if you have ever had to think about, defend, consider, justify, explain, stand up for or attempt to hide your race, language, sexual orientation, nationality, gender, faith or some other aspect of who you are, I'm guessing the learning spaces you create help ensure everyone is valued, safe and respected. Your experiences negotiating who you are in a world that might not always honour you, informs the ways you unleash learning for everyone. This might not show up in any manual, standard practice or curriculum you're expected to follow: your life informs your practices.

The same is true for other aspects of your life. When you can say no, when you stand in the center of conflict with others, when you create a life for yourself filled with balance, healthy people and choices, and when you make decisions that help you connect to your courage, the ways you unleash learning for *everyone* will expand in powerful and important ways.

While this book is designed to help you to bring out the best in what is possible for your learners, I want to remind you that who you are matters. Teaching, presenting and professional development is much more than content knowledge and curriculum strategies. While this book will help you unleash learning for *everyone*, so will the life you create for yourself. I want to encourage you to get healthier, develop more balance, face your fears, end any chaos in your life, and critically examine the power and privilege your race, gender, sexual orientation, languages or nationality affords or hampers.

By fully embracing your life, not only will you unleash learning for everyone, you will also be an important example for us all.

What is your purest intention?

In many countries, states, regions and districts, teaching is being narrowed into specified frameworks, standards and high-stakes testing. For individuals engaged in professional development, there is sometimes specific curriculum that must be adhered to. In many learning contexts, it is easy for educators to see themselves as a complier to the system, to the latest standards movement, or to a curriculum that one is working with.

Yet, you are reading this book because you want to unleash learning for *everyone* — regardless of the system you are working in, you see yourself as a builder, rather than a complier. You have specific intentions, goals, desires and outcomes for the work you do, and these intentions go beyond the system you are working within.

The 40 strategies in this book are provided to support all your students to lift the weights, but they are not intended as another item for you to comply with. You have great gifts to share. You have clear intentions. My hope is that this book will serve you, rather than be one more thing you need to comply with.

How to use this book

To get the most out of this book, I would suggest you first read its entirety. As you read, you will see that many of the 40 strategies overlap, intersect or might even seem to be similar to others, expressed in different ways. They are designed with this intention.

From there, you can decide which sections you need, and can return to them often. To help you think about the many aspects of learning, the book is divided into three sections:

Part I: Prepare

This section will provide you with strategies to use as you prepare for your learning session. Effective preparation is the key to ensuring learning is unleashed during each lesson.

Part II: Unleash learning

This section will help you think about the opening, middle and closing of the class, staff development, presentation and training session you will be running, and will provide you with specific ways to unleash learning throughout each session.

Part III: Reflect

This section will offer you strategies for thinking about your practice and the ways to make effective changes. Making changes based on your reflection processes is an important way to continue to unleash learning for *everyone*.

UNLEASH LEARNING: STRATEGIES TO UNLEASH LEARNING FOR ALL

Let's review a few things before we begin:

- You have agreed to let go of the story in your head.

- You are thinking like a coach, personal trainer or even a conductor of a symphony rather than a "teacher".

- You are reminded that learning happens each time all of your students lift the weights (yes, all!).

- You know that who you are matters.

- You know your intentions matter.

- You don't see this book as a manual to comply with, but rather a tool to support your purest intention of your work.

Okay, let's get busy!

NOTES

>> If you watch a play, listen to an orchestra or see a great performance, it can look effortless. But behind the scenes, what looked effortless was created through careful and effective preparation. The same is true for learning. A great class, presentation or learning event, properly planned for, can unleash learning for *everyone* in ways that feels effortless for all learners. To make this happen requires a different kind of preparation, one that suggests you think about all aspects of the learning session you are going to conduct, and plan it through from multiple learning vantage points. If you want to truly unleash learning for *everyone*, you will need to strategically, mindfully, consistently and intentionally create the conditions where everyone is lifting the weights throughout the session. On the following pages you'll find strategies to consider as part of your preparation process.

PART I
>> PREPARE

1. Lose your voice

You wake up one morning and you realize you don't have a voice. You drink some water, hot tea, take medication but, alas, your voice has disappeared. Although you know you are not feeling great, and the best thing to do is to stay in bed, you simply can't miss the class, presentation, or staff development session you need to lead. What do you do?

Imagining this scenario, make a list of 10 strategies that you could use that would still allow you and your learners to have a successful session. Be specific.

Strategy_____

Strategy_____

Strategy_____

Strategy_____

Strategy_____

Strategy_____

Strategy_____

Strategy_____

Strategy_____

Strategy_____

These strategies, and I'm sure you could come up with many more, are a great way to get you to think about lifting the weights. I'm not hoping that you will lose your voice or that you will sit at a desk and not talk at all. But by thinking about losing your voice, you can think through additional ways to get learners to lift the weights. You and your voice are important, but using these strategies in the service of learning, more than in the service of teaching, will help all your learners lift the weights.

HINT:

As you are preparing for your learning session, consider some of the 10 strategies you came up with if you lost your voice. I'm hoping they include the items I listed on page 15. By strategically embedding these strategies as you prepare, you can confidently ensure that learning will be unleashed for *everyone* during the session.

HOW TO LOSE YOUR VOICE WITHOUT LOSING IT

1. Create your presentation, or lesson plan. After you have created it, review your 10 strategies for how to continue if you lost your voice. Strategically embed these strategies into your presentation. For example, students will read to each other, or you will have a question already written on PowerPoint and students will individually record their answers.

2. If you are using PowerPoint, look at one of your slides where you want to embed one of these strategies. Go to "Notes Page" and put these strategies in as notes to yourself so you don't forget to use them.

3. If you are a teacher with your own classroom, place the 10 strategies on a wall so you will remember to use them on a regular basis. If you find yourself reverting to doing all of the weight lifting, these 10 strategies will quickly remind you on ways to pass the weights back to your learners.

2. Set yourself up for success

The goal of a conductor is to get the orchestra to play the symphony. To do this, the conductor sets up the ensemble prior to the musicians coming in. He or she ensures the music stands are placed in the correct position, that musicians' chairs are in the perfect position and strategically decides where everyone sits. The conductor ensures the stage is set up to allow the orchestra to reach its optimal performance while on stage. What the conductor doesn't do is say, "Hey folks, sit wherever you want to sit", or in the middle of practice ask the orchestra to move their chairs or set up during the session. Everything is set up ahead of time, in a way that ensures the orchestra can play successfully for the entire session. Simply put, the conductor sets everything up for success.

Setting yourself up for success means being proactive and ensuring you are ready to begin well before learners walk into the learning space. It means thinking through all aspects of the session you are about to run and making sure all components are set up for the best outcomes.

Some people worry that this means they are being a "control freak", or that learners may feel uncomfortable or unable to make decisions. I would suggest that while some might see a conductor as a "control freak", they instead see themselves as a master at their craft whose intention is to bring out the best of the symphony.

So, to unleash learning for *everyone*, set yourself up for success from the start.

HINT:

As you prepare for your session, create a list of all the things you need to do (such as setting up the tables, writing the agenda, setting up the technology) prior to the session. Strategically setting yourself up for success is one of the most essential things you can do to unleash learning for *everyone*.

TIPS TO SET UP FOR SUCCESS

▶ Create a seating plan that strategically, mindfully and respectfully places students in locations that bring out the best possible outcomes.

▶ Get to the room early to ensure the session is set up in the way that supports your vision and your students' success.

▶ Set up the room in the exact way you believe will ensure for success for your learners. For example, this often means not sitting a learner next to their best friend or someone who also likes to speak a lot.

▶ Have your directions agenda and instructions written on the board, PowerPoint, overhead or poster before learners enter the room.

▶ Close doors, open windows, adjust the temperature and deal with any issues that might cause a distraction during the session.

▶ Have handouts already on desks or learning spaces, so that everyone is ready to go from the start.

▶ Understand the parts of the session that might interrupt learning (moving into groups, people coming in late, or other activity changes) and put systems in place to prevent or minimise these interruptions or distractions.

3. Surround them with it

I was watching television recently and there was an advertisement for a new TV series soon to be aired. I had never heard of the show before and didn't take much notice of it. Later that day, I noticed two buses drive by with an advertisement for the same TV series. While walking home, I noticed two billboard advertisements for the TV series. That evening I was looking over a few webpages, and lo and behold, information on this TV series came up again. In a matter of a few hours, I was made aware of this TV show (whether I was interested or not).

While we may not have the same budgets as major advertising agencies, we can take an important lesson from what they are doing. For our learners, no matter what the content, a great way to unleash learning is to immerse them with the content.

Think of it this way. If you teach at a university, you might only have your students a few times a week. If you are giving a talk or running a professional learning session, you might only have the group for a few hours. If you are a high school teacher, you might only have students for one hour per day. If you are a primary school teacher, while you might work with students for the entire day, you only explore certain topics for short periods of time. Because every minute matters, and you want to ensure the moments you have with your students are moments where they are lifting the weights, surrounding them with the content is essential.

Often, the learning that students are engaging in is new for them. Maybe they are learning new terms, ideas, concepts or practices, and you want to ensure they develop deep learning on these items. Maybe you want them, much like the new TV series, to be inundated with these new ideas, terms, concepts or practices so that they are best able to lift the weights. Yet, so often I walk into learning spaces, or conference forums, and nothing is on the wall. The canvas of these learning spaces has nothing on the walls! It is like an advertising campaign that only takes place on billboards in certain parts of the city.

Remember, you are reading this book because you are looking for ways to ensure learning, deep learning, is unleashed for *all* of learners. For deep learning to take place, you know learners must lift the weights over and over again. And because you only have short periods of time with your learners, you need to use every resource you have to get them surrounded with the important, life changing and critically important learning experiences. Not only do you want them to be **lifting the weights**, but you also want them surrounded with the "dream factory" of your classroom. The walls are a critical resource that helps shift your classroom from a "fact factory" into a dream factory.

HINT:

As part of your preparation, consider ways you can surround your learners with the main ideas of the session. If you are a classroom teacher, this will mean mindfully setting up your classroom with materials that unleash learning. If you are a presenter, you might think of a picture, handout or items you can put on the floor, walls or even the ceiling. Consider surrounding students with these ideas as an important strategy and one to work with as part of your preparation process.

HOW TO USE THE WALLS

1. Consider the main outcomes, ideas, concepts, or frameworks you want your learners to gain from your time together.

2. Find posters, pictures, symbols or other displays that represent these intentions and put them on the walls.

3. What phrases, words, concepts or ideas are most essential to the learning? Create a few quick posters that have these words, concepts or ideas on them. For example, if I were running a session with a group of teachers that focused on this book, I would have one large poster on the wall that says "It's all about lifting the weights!" Actually, I would have this quote and photos of this idea on posters throughout the room.

4. Be strategic about where you locate items. Maybe there are key terms that you want you learners to use while they are lifting the weights. Could you put them on the ceiling, above where they are sitting? Or, could you put post-it notes on their seats, or desks? Or put these posters, words, quotes and images in direct view of where they are looking most of the time?

5. What about the entrance of the lecture, classroom or professional development series? Could you put a quote, key concept or idea on a poster that students have to walk over to get into the room?

6. Do you have an online forum that your learners use? Many of these learning forums let you create personal background images. What images can you put on these online learning spaces that will surround your students with the main concepts, ideas or frameworks you are having them engage in?

7. Do your learners follow you on Facebook or Twitter? Could you start posting the main ideas, topics, and experiences on these locations and see if you can get individuals to respond and engage in these locations? You might consider following me on Facebook or Twitter to see how I engage with these practices.

4. Speak mindfully

» Let's try an experiment. Tomorrow, I would like you to replace the expression "you guys" with "you girls" throughout the day. For example, instead of saying, "Can you guys hear me?" say, "Can you girls hear me?". Or instead of "I need you guys to get your books out" use "I need you girls to get your books out". After you have done this experiment for the entire day, report back what happens at **william@williamdejean.com** Let me know the reactions, responses or any kind of feedback you get from this.

Words **reflect** what we think and **impact** what we think. Words let us know who is included and who is not. Words have the alchemic power that, when used mindfully, can assist, transform and enlighten yourself and others.

For example, when I say the word "family", what image or images come to mind? Did you see a single woman raising her children? What was the race of the family you saw? Were gay or lesbian couples included in the images? What story did you see when it came to the word family? How inclusive was your vision?

If we are used to being included (we see ourselves on TV, our elective officials looks like us, our teachers look like us, we open textbooks and find our backgrounds included, people in leadership are like us) we often take it for granted. If we are often excluded, it can be disorienting, shocking, refreshing and liberating to be included, seen, recognized and honoured.

And for those who are included regularly, the inclusive language, the painting of reality that includes us all, is just as important as the topic we think we are there to learn. I believe that in order for people to participate in our world, it is essential that they develop empathy, awareness, respect, connection and curiosity for people who come from communities different than their own.

So what words do you use to include everyone when giving directions? How do you explain family, for example? Do you tell students to tell their parents, as if that is the only possibility for your learners' lives? What about husband and wife? Who is included in what you say and who is not?

Words have an alchemic property to them. They can help us transform or move into a new direction, become conscious of different kinds of possibilities, or begin to paint a reality that we might create for ourselves. Words help us know we matter. Words like "thank you", "nice job", "I am inspired by you" are as important to learning as any strategy you can use to support people to lift the weights. Your words matter!

HINT:

Speaking mindfully is something to consider as part of your preparation process. Write down notes for yourself. Embed mindful language into your talk or lesson plan. Proper planning will help create a mindful session.

›› THINGS TO THINK ABOUT DURING YOUR PREPARATION

▶ Ensure your directions, both written and spoken, include women and men.

▶ Think through your entire session, ensuring you replace "hey guys" with more inclusive language.

▶ Teach or remind learners of specific ways to recognise each other respectfully.

▶ Work to ensure everyone is recognized for his or her strengths and accomplishments, rather than focusing on the same people in a session.

▶ When giving critical feedback, focus on the feedback, not the person.

▶ Find ways to use words that include, uplift and inspire.

5. Diversify

As you become increasingly mindful of the words you use, please also become mindful of your learning resources. Your learning resources, much like your language, paint a reality for your learners. It is much easier to dream of the possibilities for our lives if we are surrounded by visions of diverse possibilities. If you can see yourself within these possibilities, it's easier to think, "Hey, I can do this too!".

Many people (myself included) fail to see themselves represented in schooling of any kind. We take literature classes, yet hear the same stories. We learn about history, but it's a history that doesn't talk about our community, our race, our family, our sexual orientation, our language, our background, our gender or our identities.

On the other hand, if we always see ourselves represented, there is danger of believing that our story is the only one that matters. For this reason, I believe it is essential to think, read, hear, experience, consider and learn from the perspective of different communities, races, genders, sexual orientations, backgrounds and people. There is a big world out there. Learning should help us all explore it further.

For this and many more reasons, mindfully look through your

HINT:

Remember, diversifying doesn't mean you should feel as if you have to get it all "right", or that every community you can think of is included. Rather, it is a way to ensure that the dream factory of your learning space represents, includes and makes visible the rich tapestry of who we all are.

learning materials and consider who is being represented. Look at your PowerPoint slides, reading materials, the walls of your classroom and other learning materials, and notice who is being included and who is not. Which races, languages, communities, stories, genders, families and races are being represented?

If your purest intention is to unleash learning for *everyone*, it is essential that everyone is included.

HOW TO DIVERSIFY YOUR LEARNING

▶ Examine the walls of your classroom. Which communities are represented? Who is excluded? What materials can you find to increase the representation of these stories and images?

▶ Look over your PowerPoint slides. Which images are being used? Are the images all white people? Are they all male?

▶ Examine the poems, books or other readings and consider who the authors are. Who are the main characters? Are they coming from the same community? What other authors can you find to diversify these reading materials?

▶ If you are using quotes to highlight something important, work to diversify the race, sex and nationality of those you are quoting.

6. Get more by using less

In a set period of time, our brains can only process so much information. And because you are intentionally working to create the conditions where learning can be unleashed for all your learners, it's important the information you use is put together in a way that brings out the best for everyone. That is why less is more!

Think of it this way. Have you ever sat through a presentation where the speaker showed slide after slide of detailed bullet points, with each slide filled with more and more information. You tried deeply to engage with what was taking place, but I'm guessing you only took in so much of what they were talking about, and probably forgot much of it once the session commenced.

To ensure this doesn't take place, it is essential that you

cut back on the information, resources, readings, materials and PowerPoint slides.

Rather than overwhelm your learners with too much information, the goal is to cut it back to the essence. What is it that you really want them to learn, focus on or be able to do? Throughout your presentation, lesson or learning session, look for ways to cut back.

HINT:

One way to get more by using less is to put your materials together and then cut back. You can easily edit items down once you have created them.

TIPS TO CUT BACK ON INFORMATION

The walls of your classroom: Rather than overwhelm your learners with information on the walls, consider cutting back so that the main ideas, themes, learning or key words are focused on the walls. Our brain can only handle so much information.

PowerPoint slides: Replace bullet points with a few key phrases or sentences. Or better yet, replace the information with a picture that captures the main message, theme or idea. Find ways to convey the main points in the most direct, concrete and accessible way.

Handouts: If you create your own handouts, ensure they are not filled with too much information. It is easy for learners to get overwhelmed, or not be able to focus on the main learning items if the page is filled with too much information. Replace key ideas with images. Break the information into chunks. Take out unnecessary words.

7. Replace it with a picture

Many companies have a simple yet powerful logo that creates emotion, understanding and brand recognition. Your learning space can do the same thing by replacing text-saturated PowerPoint slides, documents, blog postings or lessons with pictures that help create emotion, understanding and concept recognition.

When you are putting together a presentation or PowerPoint slides, search for images online* to find visual representation of what you are working on. These images will help unleash learning for your audience, readers or students. To search, simply enter your topic, idea or concept into your search engine, and click "images". If resulting images do not capture the concepts or ideas you are working with, simply refine the search terms until you find an image you like. Not only will you find great images, you will also have an opportunity to think through the concepts you are working with in new ways!

The great thing about looking at your topics through an image search is it can help you capture, conceptualise or think about the ideas you are working with and, in turn, help you find images, symbols or pictures that will help your learners as well. For example, if you have a PowerPoint slide filled with lines of information, replace the information with one image that represents the content. Or maybe you have a learning document you will be using throughout a six-week session with your group. Find a picture that symbolizes the topic of the series and put this on your document. Use it throughout the series on documents, PowerPoint slides, over posters, and so on. Replacing a lot of text with an image is a great way to unleash learning for everyone.

*It's important to remember that there are often copyright agreements with images sourced from the web. If you are a classroom or university teacher, it's not a problem to use these images for your work. If you are charging for your services, find a paid service like www.istock.com where you can purchase images.

REPLACING IT WITH A PICTURE

- Look at a PowerPoint slide you have developed and see if you can find one solid image that can represent that slide. Once you find it, delete the information and replace it with the picture (make sure it fills the entire slide!).

- Consider your class, staff development series or presentation like a brand. What image can you use to brand that session so people will understand the big picture?

- Look at a document that you have developed, which your learners use in the session. Considering the main idea of the document, do an online image search, or use a photograph you have taken, and insert one great image on the top of the document.

- If you are teaching your students for a period of time (a semester, over a few weeks or over a weekend) consider the main topic to be discussed during your sessions, and find an image or symbol to represent that topic. Use that image and symbol throughout the series. For example, if I was running a series on Unleash Learning for All!, I would have a picture of a weightlifter on the PowerPoint slide and posters throughout the room. I would revisit this image over and over again.

- If you use a blog for your students, include a picture that helps the learners conceptualise your ideas. To see how I use pictures in my blog, check out **www.williamdejean.com/blog**

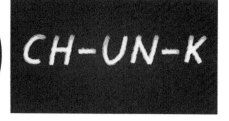

8. Chunk your instructions

If you work with a personal trainer, that trainer has a plan for your session. Rather than provide you with the plan and saying, "Go for it, you can now do it on your own", the trainer breaks down the entire session into small chunks of the plan with you. For example, the personal trainer might first have you do a few rounds on the leg machine. Next the trainer will move you to a short set working your biceps. And on and on it goes. By chunking the sessions, the trainer ensures you work strategically through each part of the program. If he or she sees that a certain part isn't going well, the trainer can quickly amend the program to ensure your muscles are firing in the exact way that will provide you with maximum success.

To get the same effect throughout your learning session, it is essential that you chunk your instructions. That is, rather than provide a bullet list of items that you want your learners to work through, consider showing just one instruction that they need to complete. From there, you might have your students speak with their partners about what they have completed before giving students the next instruction.

For many people, learning breaks down when too many instructions are provided at once. When this happens, some people or groups end quickly, and that is when disruptions occur.

HINT:

If your learning session has instructions for your learners, it is essential you craft the instruction ahead of time. Nothing interrupts learning than instructions that are not clear or are given all at once. By planning for this, ahead of time, you are ensuring success for everyone.

To avoid this, look at your directions and find ways to chunk them into smaller sections, so you can ensure everyone is lifting the weights throughout each section. You will have to think through all aspects of your session, and break them into smaller chunks.

TIPS ON CHUNKING

▶ If you use a tool like PowerPoint, review a slide that has instructions on it. Instead of showing a list of instructions, take just one and put that on its own slide. Do the same for the rest of your instructions.

▶ Rather than tell a group they have 20 minutes to work on a particular topic, watch how they are working, and then move on to the next instruction when you think time is ready.

▶ If there is a distraction in the class, review your instructions for next time. Make changes on your document, notes or PowerPoint as a reminder for your next session.

9. Break it into three

I recently went to a museum for a special art exhibition. The exhibit was broken up into different themes, with each room representing one of those themes. As you walked into the each room, there was a brief overview of the themes being represented, and then as you walked around the room, the pictures on the wall all connected to that specific theme. When you walked out of the room and into a new room, you encountered a different theme with another brief description. The rooms and the descriptions framed my thinking about the artwork and, if you will, helped unleash learning for me.

If you want to unleash learning for everyone (I know you do!),

rather than put "all the paintings in one room" I suggest you break up your presentation, lesson plan, talk, syllabus or learning event into three distinct sections.

HINT:

During your preparation period, look through your materials, and see if you can break up the session, semester or agenda into three sections. When your learners walk in the door, you will be ensuring they are set up for success.

THE POWER OF THREE

1. **PowerPoint Slides:** Look at an old PowerPoint presentation through "Slide Sorter". When you click "Slide Sorter", you will see all your slides for the entire lesson. Think of this as all the paintings of a gallery in one room.

   Now, group the slides into three distinct categories. Find a way to put items together so the lesson or presentation takes on three distinct sections. You might even consider ensuring each section has its own color so learners can distinguish between each section.

   Before you begin, let your group know that there are only three things you will be covering today. This will help learners fully engage with your "art exhibition" before they enter each section. As you give your talk or presentation, or conduct your learning session, build in time for partners to check understanding as you finish one of your sections, prior to moving into another.

2. **Agenda:** With your agenda, consider ensuring your mind map has three distinct components to it. (More on agendas and mind maps shortly.)

3. **Syllabus:** If you use a syllabus for a class, put the full schedule into three categories so students understand the three sections of the class. For example, if the class is about 20th century art, consider breaking up the full semester into three distinctive sections, with titles for those three sections. When you complete one section, provide time for students to make meaning of the section they have just completed.

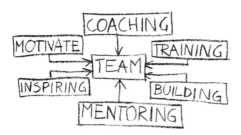

10. Use an agenda

Most textbooks have a table of contents. Many plays have a program and a description of the acts. If you rent a movie, it usually has the movie broken down into chapters, or has a trailer to view prior to watching the film. The purpose of this is to ensure that the reader, viewer or audience has a framework to engage with what will be taking place. It is the scaffolding that makes the material accessible to the participant.

The same is true for learning. Most learners want to feel safe, prepared and set up for success. Providing an agenda is a great way to support learners with a framework of what is to be expected. For example, a classroom that has an agenda on the board, or on paper for the students to see, supports the success of the student. It provides the framework that allows the learner to fully engage with what is taking place.

If you use an agenda (and I hope you do) please don't stand in front of your learners, point at an agenda and tell your students "You will learn this". It's like giving the ending to a book and

HINT:

Rather than write a list of items, like an agenda or to-do list, create a mind map that represents what the learning will be about. A mind map is a visual representation of information. Why a mind map? A mind map provides a tool to visually represent information, and helps to keep interest alive (look up "mind maps" on a web image search for examples). Remember, the brain is a problem solver. It likes to figure something out. It is curious. It likes to seek understanding and make meaning, and a mind map can help in these endeavours.

then hoping people will read it. Instead, explain to the group what the main learning intention or topic will be, and then conduct your session. For example, "Today, we will be exploring how to unleash learning for everyone," and then quickly jump into the session. When the session is completed, provide time for learners to make meaning of the experience. To do this, simply put the main idea of the lesson in the center of the mind map and make branches to the areas that will be covered. It's an easy way to create curiosity while providing a framework for success.

>> GETTING MORE FROM YOUR AGENDA

1. Write the topic on the board and break up activities or ideas as sections of the mind map.

2. Have partners read the agenda aloud to each other prior to the start of the lesson.

3. Remind learners of the agenda items throughout the session by having partners discuss aspects of the agenda that have been covered so far.

Remember, learning is unleashed every time the muscle fires. It is essential that this muscle fires the entire session, so it's vital your directions create the specific conditions for this to happen. Also, many learners (myself included) need to see the directions written down so they can fully understand what they are being asked to do.

11. Make your directions visible

Often, we think we are clear with our instructions, but learners might not fully understand or can become confused by what you are asking. When there are tasks as part of a session, lesson or presentation, optimal learning breaks down if people are confused or unclear about what they heard. I've seen really great lessons go bad the moment the educator provided verbal directions for what everyone needed to do, and everything fell apart. It wasn't that the group wasn't "motivated", or lacked interest in the work; it was that no one really understood the directions, or worse, they were spoken so quickly no one really knew what was being asked of them.

HINT:

Learning breaks down if people are confused or unclear about what you are asking them to do. Writing instructions down gives your learners the best opportunity to understand what is required of them.

TIPS TO MAKE YOUR
INSTRUCTIONS VISIBLE

- If you have important directions, ensure they are written—whether that is on the whiteboard, PowerPoint, a piece of paper or as a handout for the participants.

- While you might think your instructions are clear, your learners might need to look these instructions a few times to ensure they are on target.

- To make your instructions visible, do this ahead of your session. Putting your instructions down ahead of time will help you clarify what you are truly asking your learners to do during the session.

- Remember the importance of chunking the work. Be sure to put only a few pieces of instruction down at a time, so you can orchestrate everyone lifting the weights step by step!

12. Make it about them

You will notice that this book is all about you. As I have been writing this book, I have been thinking about you (hello!). I have been imagining the challenges you might be facing, the reasons you might be reading this book and the strategies that I believe will be most helpful to you. I'm doing this because:

1. I know you are my audience and my intention is to support you with the important work you do for our world.

2. I know that when I start to get too abstract, too distant or focus on things that don't relate to you, you might not continue reading.

With this in mind, I continue to think about you as I am writing this, and keep searching for ways to bridge these strategies to my audience: you.

Just like a personal trainer tailors a program targeted specifically for their clients' needs, unleashing learning will require that you find specific, targeted, meaningful ways to make your topic, presentation or classroom session all about your learner!

While your presentation, class or professional development session might not be focused on the lives of your learners, the goal is to find a link. That is, you might be working to unleash learning on mathematics, topics of leadership structures, or the components of a good essay with your students, and this work is not specifically about your learners. Making it about them doesn't mean changing the focus dramatically; rather, it means helping your learners see the relevance between the session and their lives.

HINT:

During your preparation, find ways to link the content and learning outcomes directly to your learners.

This will help create interest, meaning and learning. So often learners will say, or will be thinking, "Why do I need to learn this? What does this have to do with my own life?" And regardless of how passionate you are about your subject, your learners will be probably be thinking this as well. Find ways to make what they are learning about them, and you will better be able to unleash learning for *everyone*.

HOW TO MAKE IT ABOUT THEM

1. Consider how the topic (even the most abstract) connects to the lives of learners you are working with. Or consider why you think it is so essential for your students, audience, or group to unleash learning on the topic you are leading. Make a list of these connections. Find ways to make these connections explicit to your audience.

2. If your students write first (I hope they do), you can ask them questions about their lives in relationship to what is going to be studied or discussed. (See more on writing first on page 67 and prior knowledge on page 63.)

3. When you have partners discussing questions with each other, ensure they are making connections to the question or the subject. For example, if the topic of the lesson is the book *To Kill a Mockingbird*, you might ask students, describe a time when you were treated unfairly. Throughout your session, ensure students are lifting the weights on connections between the topic and their lives.

4. When you close your session, you can use the time to help your learners draw links between the session and their lives, their own thinking or their own understanding.

UNLEASH LEARNING

Your goal is to unleash learning for *everyone*. To do this will require that your actual class, presentation or professional development session is a time when all learners are lifting the weights. Each time you have all (yes, all!) of your learners...

- speak it
- teach it
- explain it to others
- draw it
- sing it
- repeat it
- summarize it

- write it
- read it to someone
- dance it
- discuss it
- question it
- engage with it
- discuss it with others

...you are ensuring that learning is being unleashed. The goal is to get that weight lifting happening throughout the learning session.

The following section provides you with strategies to unleash learning for all. It will show you how to strategically **start the session**. It will look at specific strategies for use in the **middle** of the learning session. And it will provide you strategies for **how to effectively close** the session.

These strategies are additional ways to help you and all of your learners shine!

PART II
HOW TO
>> START

HOW TO START

>> How you think about, plan and strategically start your learning session is critical to the success of you and your learners. The following strategies help set your learners up for success, help ensure time is maximized, and help to ensure learning is unleashed for *everyone* from the moment the session begins.

13. Set them up for success

It is hard to win a sporting event if you don't have the correct equipment prior to the competition. It is difficult to create beautiful orchestral music if the musicians need to find their instruments or music sheets during different parts of the performance. You can't enjoy dinner with friends if you have to run to the store three times to get supplies that are needed to cook a meal. You get the idea!

The same is true in any learning environment. Your classroom or professional learning activity can reach new levels of success if the learners are asked to be ready with *all* the materials they need before a session begins. One of the main reasons learning isn't fully unleashed is due to the high levels of interruptions that take place, including when learners are asked to get out specific learning supplies during different parts of the lesson. Setting everyone up for success is an effective way to put an end to these kinds of interruptions.

In addition, all learners want to feel safe. Setting your learners up for success (having them take out their materials ahead of time, having an agenda on your overhead, whiteboard or other device, and having the room organized ahead of time) helps learners feel safe and in control of what will be taking place.

Look through your lesson plan and figure out what your learners will need. Create a list. When students walk through the door of your presentation or talk, have the list on display (PowerPoint, overhead, whiteboard or other visual device) and ask them to get these materials out. This helps set them up for success, and helps you start the session from the get-go! Include everything; don't make assumptions that your learners will know what they need.

Things your learners might need

- pen, paper
- textbook
- paper for notes
- instructions to sit next to a partner
- their name written on paper
- computer resource
- documents they will be submitting, already stapled.

HINT:

If there are items they will need later in the session but you think having them out might be a distraction (technology, for example), ask them to put them under the desk, in the middle of the desk, or in a location that provides fast, easy assess, with little distraction. By providing a moment for your learners to get out the materials they will need for the session, you are strategically setting them up for success.

14. Build community

It doesn't matter if someone is seven or 70, if they are a learner, they will not learn from someone or engage with others until they feel safe. Many people shut down in "traditional environments", such as when the teacher arbitrarily calls on people, puts people in random groups, or indiscriminately asks the student to work with a partner they don't know or, worse, someone they've had bad experiences with outside the class.

For many individuals, a classroom environment can feel like a very unsafe space. What we might perceive as someone "not being motivated" might actually be a response to fear; that "acting out" is the guard, the caution, the safety mechanism. It's the way to ensure they will not be humiliated or made to look "dumb".

Building community is about taking the time to create a learning environment that is safe and interconnected. Building community is about getting that guard to lower enough for learners to fully engage. Building community is about letting learners know that this class is not just a subject, but rather it is the engagement of teachers, students and information that weaves together to form knowledge. Finally, building community sets the stage for learners to want to engage, connect and collaborate with each other, which are the essential conditions needed to unleash learning for all.

Many educators worry that they will not get through the units of study, materials or learning session, so they do not have time to build community. Yet, from my experience, without building community, learner's guards are up so high that few are fully taking in the session. Others see building community as a "rah-rah, mushy, touchy-feely, I-need-to-reveal-my-darkest-secrets-to-everyone" kind of experience. I believe we are all craving real experiences with each other or, at the very least, want to feel safe, connected, valued and seen. Building community is not a one time event, rather, it is a way of being together, so we can climb the mountain, explore or take the kinds of risks real learning often requires.

In a time when more and more learning is being "just put online", building community is a critical reminder about the skills needed for our world today—we don't need learners who are filled with facts, but people who can engage, open up to and connect with others. And, might I suggest, what people are longing for are experiences of community that are supportive, connected and kind.

WAYS TO BUILD COMMUNITY

‣ Provide time for the classroom community to get to know each other.

‣ Develop guidelines for how we will work together.

‣ Weave in stories, poems, YouTube clips or other resources that address respect, compassion, working together and what is possible.

‣ Sit in a circle.

‣ Get to know each other's names.

‣ Create experiences of collaboration, where students can learn to work with each other in low risk ways and then reflect on the qualities of their success.

‣ Create opportunities for partners to get to know each other.

‣ Have a seating plan or strategy (yes, even in a lecture theater, professional learning session and classroom) that brings out the best in everyone.

15. Lower the filter

There is a term I want you to remember. It's called the "affective filter". In my way of explaining it, the affective filter is the guard that we all have when we don't feel safe during learning situations. Like a castle's drawbridge, we raise our filters to protect ourselves when we don't feel safe and lower as our fear decreases. We raise and lower our filters in various ways, depending on the situation we find ourselves in. When filters are raised, we might laugh, shut down, sit in the back of the room, become the "class clown", create disruptions, be hostile or simply not engage. As educators, when we see these behaviors we sometimes form judgements or tell "stories" about our learners. We might use terms like "lazy" or "unmotivated" or label individuals. In our mind we might create stories about why this individual is behaving in these ways, without consulting them first. Often what we are seeing is fear.

If you want to unleash learning for *everyone*, you will have to lower everyone's filter. If the drawbridge is up, it is very difficult to get someone to fully engage. You will have to strategically, intentionally, mindfully and creatively create the condition that lowers the filter.

Now, to be clear, for real learning to take place, we will often experience a little fear. If we are moving out of our comfort zones, trying something new or working with new people, we are going to feel a little fear. But if that fear is too high, it will get in the way of unleashing learning. If we are too afraid, we probably won't be able to lift the weights.

For this reason, lowering the filter is not a one-time process; rather it is something to do over and over again. You will become increasingly mindful that an activity, experience or learning might bring up fear for your learners. Work to lower everyone's filter from the outset.

WAYS TO LOWER FILTERS

- Before partners share with each other, have them shake hands.

- Set up rules for groups or teams working with each other.

- Before learners give a speech, give everyone time to practise their speeches with their partner.

- Before a group works together, have them shake hands and say "you are so lucky to be working with me!"

- Before partners read to each other, let them know that they will probably make mistakes, and if they make mistakes, it's no big deal.

- Show your own humanity—share times when you have felt fear.

- Before a session, walk around the room and shake everyone's hands and say hello.

- Thank people for the great work they are doing.

- Don't speak over learners. If they are sitting down, sit with them, so you are making eye contact with everyone. Nothing is more intimidating then having someone stand over you.

- Before a group works together, have them shake hands and say "This is going to be so good!"

- Celebrate success.

- Have music playing as learners walk into the room, and use music for the moment the session is over.

16. Assign partners

How do you get a large group of students to lift the weights? How do you ensure that learning is taking place for everyone in the room? What strategy supports all learning to fully engage with the class, content and their own learning? The very best way I know to do this is to have students work with a partner.

We only can process so much information at a time. Our brains can really only focus for shorts periods of time. We all need time to think through new ideas and get support, as needed, when we don't fully understand new concepts. Working with a partner supports this, and so much more.

Your seating chart or seating plan is important to the success of this work, so consider carefully who is sitting with whom. If you are using a large lecture theater for your lesson, you can still have people sit next to a partner. The trick is to ensure people sit next to someone, or have an assigned seating location, as learners walk in. It is nearly impossible to get individuals to move or find a partner in a large lecture hall or learning space once they have already sat down.

Once you have people seated in a location that supports partner work, before the start of the lesson, ask partners to decide who is partner A or B, or make it interesting by asking them to assign who is New York or Sydney.

HINT:

As you can see, working with a partner is a great way to support all of your learners throughout the session. The key is starting your learning session with a moment when learners can connect with their partner and know they will be working with this person throughout the session. Ideally, you will have a seating plan that strategically seats people next to the partner they'll be working with. This sets everyone up for success.

GETTING PARTNERS TO WORK WITH EACH OTHER

At the start of a lesson

▶ Provide students time to write first (more on this shortly), and then invite them to share their answers with a partner.

▶ Have a list of questions that relate to the previous lesson, and ask partners to share their answers with each other. This is a great way to review previous information, and provide learners opportunities to continue to think through these concepts

▶ Have partners read the lesson's agenda on the board to each other

In the middle of the lesson

▶ When you can tell that the class is getting tired, needs a break or might need time to process the learning, ask partners to stand, and have questions on the board that they can answer in response to the learning session.

▶ During a discussion, have partners respond to each other about some of the key questions or ideas, prior to moving it to a large discussion.

▶ If learners need to give a speech or make a presentation, they can practice this with their partner and get feedback so they can make changes before the presentation.

▶ When there are instructions on the board (PowerPoint, whiteboard and so on) assign partners A and B to read the instruction to each other.

At the end of a lesson

▶ When students have written last (more on this later), have them read their responses to each other.

▶ Have partners explain the agenda that is written on the board and explain to each other what they learned.

17. Activate prior knowledge

I'm going to give you a test. It's a very high stakes test. I'm going to give you a sentence, and I want you to write down what this sentence means. There is only one correct answer, since this is such a high stakes test. Ready. The sentence is: **I ran home**. What does this sentence mean? Okay, time's up.

But wait, I want you to pass the test. More importantly, I want learning to be unleashed for you, so let's try it again. But this time I am going to have you first write about any sport you have ever played and ask you to share this information with a partner. Then I'll ask just a few people to briefly share what sports they have played. Next, I'm going to have you read the rules for playing American baseball. I'm going to show you a few film clips about baseball, with players talking about their strategies for winning the game. Finally, I'm going to show you an example of a baseball player running from third base to home base so you can see how the game works.

HINT:
Whatever strategy you use, create a bridge from the life of your learners to the materials, experience or topic they will be exploring in your lesson, workshop or presentation. For example, if you are about to study WWII, provide time for students to think about a conflict that has taken place around their own lives and the ways they have resolved that conflict. (Don't forget to have them talk with their partners after they write, and only have a few people share out loud afterwards.)

In whatever learning capacity you find yourself in, creating ways to quickly activate prior knowledge is an essential and critical tool to unleash learning for all.

Let's test you again. Please write down what this sentence means: **I ran home.**

Did you pass? Great! What was the difference this time? What supported you doing well the second time?

The two tests are a reminder that learning often has less to do with who is "smart" and who is "not smart", and more to do with the amount of prior knowledge a learner has. That is why ensuring we activate prior knowledge is an essential step in supporting learning to being unleashed for *everyone*.

So what gets in the way of activating prior knowledge? We have "taught" the materials for so long we forget that this is might be the first time our learners have engaged with the materials. We assume that our learners all have the same background or come with the same background experiences.

We have a story in our head for what students should already know when they come into our classrooms, presentations or staff development session. So, if you want to unleash learning for the people you work with, remember it's all about prior knowledge!

HOW TO ACTIVATE PRIOR KNOWLEDGE

- Have students write briefly about the ideas or topics that relate to the lesson or talk they are about to engage in.

- Ask a compelling question.

- Provide a quick survey on ideas or topics of the lesson.

- Have a list of questions that relate to the topic of the lesson and have partners respond to each other about these questions.

- Have students read a poem or listen to music that connects to the themes or ideas the lesson will be about.

- Provide opportunities for learners to reflect on topics, themes, ideas or lessons to review their knowledge prior to discussions.

18. Ask a compelling opening question

The first minutes of your learning session, presentation or class are critical. These minutes are your opportunity to quickly get buy-in, create interest, eliminate distractions and get the most out of the learning session. It is impossible to unleash learning when the first few moments of a session are awkwardly spent trying to get everyone's attention or attempting to settle everyone down.

In addition, your learners might have come from another class, sat through a speaker prior to yours, or returned from a break talking with others and have their minds on other things. The session you are about to run is important and you need to quickly get everyone in the right state of mind.

So start your session by asking a compelling opening question.

A compelling opening question is a question that is going to tap into your learners' lives and help them connect to your presentation or class. It is a question that garners interests and creates excitement, curiosity or strong emotions. It is a question you know most of our learners will be able to respond to in some way. It is also a question that can help activate prior knowledge for all of your students.

When you get your group seated, simply ask your compelling opening question in a dramatic way. Ask it slowly, with a lowered

HINT:

It's important to ensure that the compelling question you ask is respectful, risk free and brings out the best in everyone. Once you have captured their interests and connected to your session, quickly show your learners the topic of the presentation, lesson or classroom session, and begin.

voice. Ask it in a way that captures the group's attention.

If I were giving a one-hour presentation to a large group about this book, some of the compelling opening questions I might use could be:

1. Have you ever sat through a boring class, lecture or learning session? If so, please stand up.

2. With a show of hands, how many people in here have ever gotten in trouble for talking in class?

The key is to find a question that peaks interest, that people can relate to and that taps them into what the learning session is about—and gets them lifting the weights by standing or raising hands. If you would like to see this strategy in action, please watch the first few minutes of my TEDx talk at: **www.williamdejean.com/tedx**

ASKING COMPELLING QUESTIONS

- activates prior knowledge
- quickly captures everyone's attention
- connects learners' experiences with your class or presentation
- makes the most of your instructional time.

19. Always write first

Have you ever been in a learning environment where the teacher randomly calls on people? The game is played like this. The teacher asks the class a specific question and randomly starts picking students to answer the question. Many students quickly look to the ground believing that if they do not make eye contact with the teacher, they will not be chosen. One or two students, who are particularly good at the game or know the answer the teacher wants, raises his or her hand. Once the teacher selects a student, a discussion begins between the teacher and that student, and the rest of the class disengages.

Another game goes like this. The teacher asks a question and goes in order around the classroom to answer the question. The students, waiting to answer the questions, are focused solely on their answers and not listening to the responses of their classmates. Once they have answered the questions, from relief, they stop paying attention. In both of these examples, very few students are lifting the weights. They are simply playing the game of "schooling".

There is another way.

To set up opportunities where learning can be unleashed for *everyone*, start your session by presenting a general question that addresses the topic of the class (use the overhead projector, white board or PowerPoint), and provide students with time to record their answers.

Writing first gives learners:

❱ an opportunity to lift the weights

❱ time to think

❱ an opportunity to activate prior knowledge

❱ a safe space to consider their own knowledge and thinking.

HINT:

Writing first is a quick and easy way to start your talk, lesson or learning session.

TIPS ON WRITING FIRST

▶ Limit the writing to 2-3 minutes.

▶ Make the question relate directly to your students' lives.

▶ Use questions and the writing as a bridge to connect the topic to students' lived experiences.

▶ Provide time for students to share answers with each other.

▶ Call on a few people (no more than three) to share their response to the entire group.

▶ Once this is complete, you can introduce learners to the topic that will be explored.

PART II

>> WHAT TO DO IN THE MIDDLE

WHAT TO DO IN THE MIDDLE

>> The middle of your session is when learning is being unleashed and things are moving full speed ahead. It is when the life changing, transforming and inspiring work takes place. It's the time when you are strategically, mindfully, intentionally and consistently supporting everyone to lift the weights so that learning can be unleashed for *everyone*. As such, consider the following strategies in the middle of your session, to bring out the best in what is possible for all of your learners.

20. Read to a partner

Here's how the game of learning is sometimes played out when it comes to reading. The teacher reads to the group. While some learners are engaged, the rest of the group pretends to be listening or is thinking instead about other things. The students are nodding and smiling while the teacher is reading, but there is really no way to know if they are lifting the weights. It's not their fault. It's just that they have a lot going on in their lives and have been sitting for a very long time, and might have something that is much more important to think about than what the teacher is reading to them.

The other way the game is played is that students read something to themselves, silently. You pass out an article and ask the students to read it. It all looks so good: there is quiet in the class,

all eyes are the page of text and everyone seems to be reading. But are they learning? Are they engaging with the reading? How do you know any comprehension is taking place?

To get them to lift the weights, have your students read the article with a partner. That's right, together. Reading to a partner is a great for:

▶ poems

▶ shorter articles

▶ starting a chapter in a book

▶ reading a handout

▶ getting students to read an assignment you have passed out.

HINT:

Because you have set your learners up for success, and started the lesson by assigning learners to partners, you can quickly move into having those partners read to each other throughout the session.

READING WITH PARTNERS

▶ Find a short reading (three pages or less) that you want to use with your learners.

▶ Have partners read out loud, alternating per paragraph.

▶ While they are reading or following with the reading, they are asked to highlight or underline what stands out as important.

▶ When they are done, have them write the main message of the article, in 30 words or less.

▶ Have partners share their words with each other.

▶ Ask for two or three students to read their summaries out loud.

21. Have them take notes

Writing to learn is a powerful tool to help unleash learning for *everyone*. This is because as we write, we are thinking through our own ideas. We might think we already know what we know, but we often actually discover our learning through the writing process. It is one of the many reasons I encourage you to have your learners writing to learn. Not only does writing help everyone think through his or her own learning, it is also a quick way for you to monitor who is lifting the weights. When a pen is touching the paper, you know learners are lifting the weights. It's really as simple as that.

That is why I encourage you to have your learners take notes throughout your session. Much like a reporter during a press conference, creating an environment where *all* learners are actively taking notes throughout the session adds an important weight lifting opportunity.

HINT:

The idea is not for your learners to try to write down everything you or others say, or everything that is on the presentation or the class materials used. Rather, the idea is to create an environment where learners are lifting the weights through writing. While writing first and last (strategies 19 and 36, respectively) are great writing-to-learn strategies, writing throughout the session is another important component of that process. For example, building in note taking combined with opportunities for partners to share their notes with each other, creates a great way to support all of your learners to lift the weights throughout your learning session.

Whatever kind of note-taking system you choose to use, the key is to ensure people are using it. This means you might need to build in opportunities for everyone to take notes. For example, during a large group discussion, if you want to ensure everyone is lifting the weights, make sure your learners have their notes out, and provide time for them to record what they are hearing in the discussion. You can even stop in strategic parts of the session to ask partners to share their notes with each other (out loud!).

>> BUILDING NOTE TAKING INTO YOUR SESSION

1. Ensure everyone has notepaper ready before a session begins.

2. Throughout the session, continue to remind everyone to take notes.

3. If there is a large group discussion going on, encourage everyone to take notes on the main points of the discussion.

4. If you are having learners watch a film, listen to a speaker or podcast, have them take notes on the most important ideas.

5. Before you give a talk, encourage everyone to take notes. Plan time where you stop and ask partners to discuss their notes with each other.

22. Pass out the weights

You know that to unleash learning you have to mindfully, consistently, strategically, intentionally and continually support your learners to lift the weights with the information, materials or experiences you have prepared. You know that every time you get your students to write, speak, discuss, read to someone else, teach it, explain it, say it out loud, the weights are in your learners hands, and each time they lift them, learning is being unleashed. Every time you get them to lift the weights, you are helping the firing of the muscles of their hearts, minds and spirits. Each time the heart, mind or spirit fires, learning is unleashed. And the more they lift the weights, the deeper the levels of learning will stay with them.

Yet, because of the story in our head, it can be easy to revert back to having just a few students lifting the weights, or to not see through the lenses of those students who are sitting back and not really engaging. We can easily revert to the teacher story and start talking, talking, talking, without ensuring students are truly learning, learning, learning. When we do all the teaching, talking or explaining, the weights are in our hand, and not the hands of our learners.

During your presentation, staff development session or class, look critically to see who is lifting the weights. If you notice that few students are lifting the weights, you can quickly find ways to pass out the weights to your learners. You might ask everyone to stand, read the agenda to their partners, or share their notes with someone in the room. Or you might notice you are doing all of the talking, and quickly stop and enact strategies that pass the weights back to your learners. As you become a master at ways to unleash learning, you will increasingly notice who is not lifting the weights and be able to adjust on the spot.

In the middle of a learning session, it can be easy to be so caught up in the session that we are not paying attention to who is lifting the weights. During the middle of your session, keep looking around the room. If you see that your plan for *everyone* to be lifting the weights isn't fully working, see if you can make some quick changes to make it happen.

Quick ways to pass out the weights

▶ Ask everyone to stand and read their notes to two or three people in the room. When they are done, ask them to return to their original seat.

▶ If you have information written on PowerPoint slides, rather than read the information to your learners, have partners read the information out loud to each other.

▶ Have learners find a partner they have not worked with before. Ask them to decide who is the "A" partner and who is the "B" partner. During the lesson, take a moment for partners find each other. Provide specific instructions for partner A and specific instructions for partner B (for example, explain in their own words what the session is causing them to think about, read assigned reading

to each other, explain the PowerPoint slides in their own words). Whenever you want to increase weight lifting, simply ask partners to find each other and add another set of tasks for them to quickly complete.

THINGS TO CONSIDER

▶ Throughout the lesson, consider who is lifting the weights. Look through the lenses of gender, race, language, ability, age, and so on. What communities are weight lifting and which are not?

▶ For what percentage of your session do you have all of your learners fully lifting the weights?

▶ How much of the session are you talking?

▶ When learners are working in small groups, which students in these groups are lifting the weights?

▶ Of all of your learners, who is doing the reading and writing?

▶ What strategies can you put into place to ensure the small groups are lifting the weights together?

▶ How does the set up (tables, chairs, seating charts) support or hinder all students weight lifting?

23. Draw it

There may be times when you need to read a passage to your group of learners. Or maybe you really need your learners to read something individually because that would best suit the outcomes you have in mind. Or maybe you have small teams working together, and you want one person to read to the small teams because this best meets your outcomes and intentions. So, to ensure that learning is unleashed for everyone during these moments, have your learners draw what is being read.

It goes like this. If you are reading out loud to a large group, or they are reading individually or with their teams, ask the learners to draw what they are visualizing from the reading. These drawings don't need to be perfect. They can be stick figures, words, symbols or small images. Good readers visualize what they are reading or hearing. Because you want learning to be unleashed in all moments, getting them to lift the weights by drawing as the reading is taking place is a great strategy to embed into your learning session.

DRAWING WITH SUCCESS

» ▶ Set your learners up for success and ensure they have all the materials they will need, such as pen and paper, so when you are ready to read, they are ready to start drawing.

▶ If they are reading a poem, handout or other document you have provided, consider having them draw on the handout itself.

▶ If you are reading a large passage to a group, stop every few minutes and ask partners to share their drawing with each other.

▶ At the end of the drawings, ask students to summarize the main message of the reading in 30 words or less.

24. Have them speak it

A quiet classroom is deeply embedded into the stories we have in our head about teaching and learning. That is, your story probably includes a classroom where only one person speaks at a time and, when learners are not speaking, it is very quiet. But if you want to really unleash learning, I suggest you need a bit of noise. I'm not talking about the kind of noise where nothing is really happening, people are talking freely about random things, or learners are discussing their weekend plans. I'm not going to get all neuroscience on you, but I will suggest that when learners *speak it, they learn it.*

Consider it this way. Have you ever read a book and thought you understood it? Maybe it was a work of fiction, and each night before you slept, you read a few chapters. You might have really loved the book, which provided a great escape and expanded your thinking. Yet, it wasn't until someone asked you about the book that you really thought about what you understood and what you did not. Just like writing first and last helps clarify the thinking of learners, speaking is an important tool that helps *everyone* lift the weights.

Here's a way to approach this. Think of a lesson, presentation, unit of study or your current class. Make a list all the important terms, ideas, pieces of information or procedures you hope your learners will truly learn—these are the key ideas, terms, concepts or understandings you hope learners will keep with them for a very long time. For example, if I were working with a group to unleash learning on the key components of this book, so they become the very best educators this world has ever seen, my list of words and ideas would include:

‣ Lifting the weights.

‣ It's all about prior knowledge.

‣ Always write first and last.

‣ When you speak it, you learn it.

▶ Set them up for success.

▶ Chunk your directions.

And because my intention is to get *everyone* to lift the weights on these ideas and key terms, I would find ways to get them to talk about these key ideas over and over again.

Remember, you are committed to strategically, mindfully, intentionally and consistently working to get learners to lift the weights, and you know to write first and last. The more you can get *everyone* to talk about these key terms and phrases, the more likely it will become so common in their language that they maintain it for a very long time.

GETTING THEM TO SPEAK IT

1. The reasons you have people sitting strategically and working with partners is so people can talk together. Ensure that after learners write first or last (more on this later), you have them share their answers.

2. If you see the energy of the group is starting to fade, ask everyone to stand up. Then ask them a few questions about the session, or have them share the agenda or something from their notes.

25. Have them teach it

Many educators share with me how they didn't fully learn something until they taught it. That is, they were very confident and competent in the area of learning they were working on, but they didn't fully learn it until they had to teach it.

Why? Because they were lifting the weights!

When you turn the tables on your learners and provide them with the opportunities, strategies, skills and events where they can teach what they are learning, you can be increasingly assured that learning will be unleashed for them.

I am not suggesting you give up your day job and simply sit down and let your learners do all the work. Rather, I'm suggesting you create opportunities where they can "teach" to others certain aspects of your session.

Let's think of it this way. If I were working to unleash learning from aspects of this book, I would strategically find ways for you to lift the weights on those sections of the book. For example, I would have you write first, activate your prior knowledge, read a section of this book to a partner, summarize it in your notes, and then I would create opportunities for you to teach the main concepts to someone else in the class session.

GETTING THEM TO TEACH IT

1. Find main ideas from your presentation, lesson or classroom session that you think are critical for your learners to remember for a long time.

2. Create opportunities for partners or small groups to work together.

3. Show the title, agenda, topic or important idea on your PowerPoint, whiteboard or other visual aid.

4. Have the partner explain, discuss or put into his or her own words the main ideas of this piece of knowledge.

26. Pay attention to who is speaking

You are strategically working to get everyone to lift the weights. You know that by getting *everyone* to speak it, you help them learn it. With that in mind, by paying attention to who is speaking, you will have a lens to consider who is weight lifting. So if you notice throughout your session or during group discussions that only a few people (maybe the same people) are speaking, then you will have a lens to consider how well you are unleashing learning for *all*.

For example, you might notice that when you ask for volunteers the same people answer. Or, when learners are working in small groups, you might see that the same people in each group are doing all the talking. This is a great opportunity to critically examine what is taking place and then put strategies into place to unleash learning for more people.

As you continue to get better at unleashing learning, you might notice in the middle of your session that you have been doing all of the talking, or that only a few people have been speaking in groups. Thinking quickly on your feet, you can immediately embed strategies to change this, such as getting everyone to stand and talk to a partner, or having them write. Alternatively, when you revise your session for next time, you can strategically embed ways to support *everyone* to speak at different times.

HINT:

Paying attention to who is speaking is a quick lens to examine learning in your session. You can then quickly make adjustments, or consider this lens when you are planning for your next learning session.

STRATEGIES TO SUPPORT SPEAKING

▶ You might find the learning groups too large. During your next session, you might make the groups much smaller or have partners working together rather than individuals working in groups. This will support more people speaking.

▶ You might find that when you ask for volunteers, you always hear from the same people. Instead, ask groups to figure out who woke up the earliest, and then invite that person to share his or her answer.

▶ You might discover that men are doing all of the talking, or certain communities never have a chance to speak because they are being silenced or interrupted by other members of the class. Look through the lens of race, gender, sexual orientation, faith, nationality, language, ability and age. Who is speaking? If learners are in groups of four, have them number off. When large discussions take place, ask for specific numbers to share their ideas to the entire class, or ask specific numbers to share within the group. This will help strategically support everyone speaking throughout the session.

▶ You might notice you have been doing all the weight lifting, and quickly decide to ask partners to read to each other the directions that you have on your PowerPoint.

27. Share power

It is impossible to unleash learning for *everyone* if only a few people are lifting the weights. This will mean a conscious, mindful approach to the work you are doing and the work your learners are doing. It will mean paying attention to who is writing, speaking, reading, explaining, teaching, discussing and engaging.

Many of us have experienced learning when power is held over us. One example of this is when the teacher does all the talking, controls the room or only responds to a few students. Or when we have worked in learning groups and a few people dominate the group interaction.

For learning to be unleashed throughout the session, power needs to be shared. This means:

▶ partners working equally together

▶ groups strategically sharing the workload

▶ students speaking as much as the teacher

▶ both men and women are being heard

▶ equal participation with learners from different backgrounds (race, gender, sexual orientation, language, nationality, ability, faith).

Sharing power, much like collaboration, is not innate. It is something to be worked on, enhanced and consistently developed. While you want to unleash learning around the content of your class, you are also helping to unleash learning about the many ways we can share power with each other.

To ensure power is shared, you will need to clearly, consistently, mindfully and proactively build in opportunities for learners to practise these endeavours together.

HOW TO SHARE POWER

▶ Put quotes, statements, and reminders around the room that focus on working together, respect, effective collaboration, diversity and listening.

▶ Provide clear instructions on how partners or groups need to work with each other before tasks begin.

▶ Proactively create seating charts that diversify who works together.

▶ Set up rules and responsibilities for group work that ensures everyone has a voice and participates equally.

▶ Provide time for individuals and groups to reflect on how well they worked together, and ways they can increase their performance.

▶ Ensure respectful language is used at all times.

▶ Constantly examine who is lifting the weights throughout the session.

28. Check for understanding

Have you ever been reading something and then your mind began thinking of other things? You might have "read" five pages, but during that time you were thinking about the long list of things to get accomplished later in the day, or what is taking place during the weekend. By the time you got to the fifth page, you realized you had no idea what you'd read and had to begin again This is the same with learners, of any age or any learning situation.

As the teacher, presenter or staff developer, you might have worked with your resources for so long that you could talk about them in your sleep. You have lifted these weights numerous times with the lesson, materials or experiences you've created, yet for your learners, this might be the first time they

have engaged with the topic, material or activity. That is why it is essential you provide time for *all* of your learners to check for understanding throughout your learning session.

There are many ways to check for understanding. The key is to embed these checks strategically in your learning. Each time your learners check their understanding, and even compare it with others, you can increase your confidence that learning is being unleashed.

HINT:

One great way to check for understanding is by working with a partner. To do this, remember to assign partners at the start of the session and ensure they are sitting next to each other.

TIPS TO CHECK FOR
UNDERSTANDING

1. **Use a questionnaire:** Create a small questionnaire that focuses on the questions that connect to the main topic of the lesson or key ideas. Embed a moment where partners who are working together each spend a minute discussing their individual answers.

2. **After a break:** If you provide breaks within your learning sessions, use the return from the break as a time to check for understanding on what took place prior to the break. Here you can use a list of questions, writing first, or have partners speak to each other about the agenda and what they have learned in the first session.

3. **In their own words:** Put up a few key ideas or phrases from the lesson and have partners explain what these key terms or ideas mean. When they speak it or teach it, they will learn it.

29. Ride the wave

Most educators want learners to be so involved in a learning situation that when it is finished, they couldn't believe the time flew so quickly. They were so engaged, that is, the weight lifting session moved so effortlessly, they didn't pay attention to the time. The session was so masterful that people couldn't believe it was coming to an end, because they were fully enveloped in the zone of learning.

To get this to happen, you are going to need to ride the wave.

Just like a wave that is about to crest and crash onto shore, you need to monitor the energy of the room, the engagement of your learners or the groups that are working, and decide, based on their energy, when to move on to the next activity or part of the session. Rather then tell your learners, "You have 20 minutes to complete this", watch the group. As people start finishing, just like a cresting wave, begin to transition into the next section.

Remember, the goal here is to get the muscles firing for the *entire* session you are leading. If half of your class has finished or is not weight lifting, it is time to move to the next session. The goal is speeding things up, not to rush them, but to ensure muscles are firing over and over again. Often the muscles stop firing during the **transition** period of our sessions because the transition period is when we lose a lot of our learners. It is when the phones come out, when people start talking or when other disruptions occur. Riding the wave is the strategy for keeping the energy of the learning session at its peak, so

HINT:

Riding the wave is about using strategies that keep the pace of learning moving in a way that ensures *everyone* is lifting the weights throughout the entire session.

all learners are lifting the weights throughout the learning session.

This will mean that you need not wait for the very last person to finish. It's not being rude; rather it's knowing that if the wave crashes to the shore while you are waiting for a few last people to finish, it will be difficult to get another wave to peak.

HOW TO RIDE THE WAVE

▶ If you have a few people still working, or groups who are finishing up, kindly, respectfully, graciously ask them to finish their thought. Ask everyone in the group, before the wave crests, to stand up. This will encourage those last few people to complete their work and join the group.

▶ If you are at a peek moment with the class, stay there by getting everyone to stand up.

▶ If you think the wave is about to crash, have the entire group stand in a circle. Ask a question and have partners speak to each other about it. Provide specific instructions prior to returning to their chairs.

▶ Consider the pacing of your talk, or specific sections. Sometimes you will need to redo your presentation because you will notice the parts of it that cause the wave to crash.

30. Have them think about their thinking

I once had a class with more than 300 people. There was a large lecture hall where students thought they would listen to me lecture each week. Later, we would meet in small tutorial groups where they thought I would talk a little more about the topics we were covering.

But since I was interested in unleashing learning, I had them moving, talking with a partner, taking notes, teaching each other and finding other ways to get them to lift the weights on the main ideas of the class.

During the fifth week of the course, a student stopped me as I was leaving the lecture theater to let me know he wasn't learning anything. He seemed panicked actually.

As I listened to him share his concerns about what he wasn't learning and how our sessions were confusing him, I realized that our class didn't look like the other classes he was taking. The "story" in his head, combined with the relationship of our class to his others, was convincing him that he wasn't learning anything. To calm his nerves, I asked him a few questions.

> How does **working with a partner** impact you as a learner?

> How does **teaching the materials to others** impact you as a learner?

> How does **writing first impact** you as a learner?

> How does **repeating key words or phrases** impact you as a writer?

After I asked him each question, his answers seemed to surprise him. The more I asked, the deeper his answers became. It was as if hearing his answers let him see his own learning. By the end of the semester, he started to recite, explain and discuss with others in the class what he was learning, and what was contributing to it.

Metacognition is the process of thinking about our own thinking. From an unleashed learning perspective, helping our students think about their thinking in relation to their learning is helpful for many reasons. It assists them to create purpose and meaning for the ways we are conducting the sessions. More importantly, it helps them think about their thinking on the topic or learning at hand. Without metacognition, learning can be like a train that simply follows the track, moving from one station to the next; there's no reflection or meaning making. In many ways, metacognition places learners in the center of their own learning, and asks them to think critically about it.

For metacognition to happen, the questions we ask learners are important. For example, please don't ask if they like taking notes or working with a partner. Instead, ask about the critical components of the learning in relationship to their own learning. Learners who start thinking about their own learning

might even feel empowered as they consider how they are lifting the weights and what this means to their own success.

HINT:

If you are running a course or meeting with learners over a given period of time, having learners thinking about their own thinking can be useful to help create additional success. Just like a weightlifter reflecting on his or her weight lifting processes, learners who reflect on their own thinking can help find greater levels of success and meaning.

KEY QUESTIONS

How did _____ impact you as a learner?

How did _____ impact you are a writer?

How does _____ impact you as a participant?

How does _____ impact you as a reader?

31. Get them to repeat it

I recently bumped into a former student. We hadn't seen each other in almost four years. When he approached me he started saying things like, "It's all about lifting the weights!"; "Always write first and last"; "It's all about prior knowledge." When I asked him how he remembered that after so many years, he simply said, "We repeated it all the time." I then asked him how he was using that knowledge he learned in our class with the work he does today. His list of ways was endless.

When you have your learners repeat key terms, phrases or ideas that are essential for the learning session, you are having your learners lift the weights on these concepts. It's like every time they come to your gym you will be

sure that your learners are lifting specific weights, no matter what the session is about, so you can ensure they gain muscle. Getting your learners to repeat it (over and over again!) is an easy way to ensure their muscles are firing. And you know how it works: the more often those muscles fire, the more often you are supporting learning being unleashed.

The key here is not to get them to just repeat everything. This is not about rote learning. I'm suggesting that if you can find a list of key terms, ideas or outcomes you want to unleash for your learners, getting them to repeat them with you is an important weight lifting strategy.

The secret is to get them to repeat the most important, most essential, most critical ideas that are a part of your lesson, presentation or learning session. After they have understood these concepts, you can take out the key word and have them fill in the blanks for their repetitions.

To make this work, consider the main ideas or concepts that you will be covering, and that you want to unleash for your students. Come up with a few quick phrases or sentences that are key to the learning. These main terms or phrases will form what you want them to repeat with you.

Here's an example. If I were running a session on this book, and I had you for a few sessions, I would write down the main ideas, terms or concepts I want you to remember. I know I will get you to write about it, speak with your partner, read to others, and lift the weights in many ways on these concepts. But I also know that getting you to repeat these ideas will also help unleash the learning for you.

I would say something like:

"You are going to think I am a little strange, but this session will be getting you to 'lift the weights'. And that only by getting you to 'lift the weights' can you and I be sure you really learn. So you will quickly see it's all about 'lifting the [pause].'"

Now the first time you do this, you will get some weird looks, and many people won't fill in that blank. You might think, "Wow they do think I am strange", lose confidence and not do it.

So you should do it again.

"Let me try that again. I know you think I'm a little out of it, but maybe you are a little tired

this morning. You will see it's all about 'lifting the [pause] ____ .'"

Often a few more people will repeat it. The goal is to get *everyone* to repeat it—you will need to do it a few times until they are with you, and everyone is acting weird and are loud about it together.

For every session with this group, I want you to start with your key term, and then add a few more. And I want you to leave out the

HINT:

How do you do this if you are giving a one-hour talk? Simply find a few key terms or phrases that are most essential to your talk. You can then start the talk with these key terms, get a few repetitions in the middle and finish with the same terms of repetition at the end. They will appreciate you for being different and will be tuned in to the main ideas of your presentation.

main word or idea so they have to fill it in. By the end, you'll have a list of terms that you can use, which your learners are using each time. You might think it's odd, but this repetition works. And don't worry about the looks you get the first time—the learners will come on board!

MY FAVORITE REPETITIONS

"It's about lifting the _____!"

"Always write _____ and _____ !"

"It's all about prior_____!"

"When you speak it, you _____!"

"When you are thinking about your thinking it is meta - _____ ."

be a time when the teacher or presenter loses control.

The key to getting all learners moving is to create mindful, meaningful and carefully planned opportunities for movement to take place, and to consider how using movement will help *everyone* lift the weighs.

32. Get them to move

Getting your learners to move is essential. It will help reinvigorate learners who are often sitting for long periods of time. It will help add interest, because it is not something they are used to doing in a learning session. If used strategically, it will help them focus on the main points of the learning. And, finally, it's a great way to ensure *everyone* is lifting the weights!

Sitting is often deeply embedded into the stories we have about learning. Some people (not you because you are reading this book!) will worry that getting learners to stand, move and learn will be difficult or, worse, will

> ## HINT:
>
> Getting learners to move is an easy way to quickly get interest, keep the energy moving, help people stay focused and, ultimately, unleash learning for everyone!

HOW TO GET LEARNERS MOVING

▶ You have set yourself and your group up for success. They are sitting with partners and have written first. After they have written first, ask everyone to stand and share their answers with their partners. When they are done, ask them to sit down.

▶ You have put a few questions on the PowerPoint slide for partners to discuss. Have them stand up during that conversation and sit down when they are done.

▶ Create a walk and talk. To do this, simply have questions that you would otherwise put on your PowerPoint and type them up ahead of time. Give the questions to partners. Have them walk around the room and discuss their answers to the questions. When they are finished, have them sit back down and record in their notes what the conversation prompted them to think about.

▶ As a way to begin your session, ask everyone to stand up and read together the title of the learning session.

▶ If you notice that people's attention is fading, a few cell phones have come out, or a few people are talking, have everyone stand up. It's a great way to get the attention back to the present, ride the wave, and to quickly embed some weight lifting work. In that moment, have them talk with a partner about something that relates to the session.

33. Focus on the best of the best

Your goal is to help your learners reach success. You want to help bring out the best in who they are, what they can do, learn, become and achieve. You want them to be transformed by the class, talk or session they have with you, and you hope the experience will remain with them for a very long time. You have important gifts to share and believe that the session you are running is essential, important and life changing.

Yet, it can be very easy to forget all of this the moment you see people texting during a learning session, the moment you are grading assignments, the moment students come late to your class, or the moment someone unmindfully asks a lot of questions that interfere with everyone's learning. Over time,

these little problems seem to take up most of your energy as you react to these issues rather than engaging with the important work at hand.

To ensure your energy is concentrated on the positive outcomes you are working towards, focusing on the best of the best will help you consider the learners you have and the direction you want them to go.

Here's how it can work.

Show examples: If you are asking learners to craft an essay, create a product or give a presentation, show the best that you have as an example. For instance, some of your learners will have no idea what a product might look like, so show some of the best examples you can find. This not only focuses on the best of the best, but because you have set the bar high, you will be encouraging your learners to jump right over it.

Focus on what is working: You might notice on occasion that a few individuals are looking at their phones or engaging in side conversations. It can be easy to point this out, and bring the entire learning group's morale down. Instead of pointing this out to everyone, discuss what is working well in the class. Ask learners to write down comments about what is working and share these comments with each other. If you want to create success, focus on success over and over again. Point it out. Talk about it. Celebrate it. Over time, you and your learners will create more and more of it.

Write great comments: When I was an English teacher, grading essays was challenging. I spent hours reading assignments and making comments on what wasn't working with their writing. After a few years, I realized that I needed to spend more time focusing on what was working with the majority of the essays, and let the students know about this. I did write comments highlighting areas of improvement, but I spent just as much time pointing out areas of strength. When I returned the assignments, I had students take notes on my comments on the positive aspects of the best writing with suggestions for everyone as to how to write like that. By writing great comments and focusing on the best of the assignments, my students were able to know how to improve and what great writing looked like.

If you are giving feedback on assignments, be sure to find what they are doing well and write comments on this. As part of your feedback to the entire group, be sure to explain the features of the great assignments. For your learners who didn't do as well, this will help them see areas in their own work where they can improve for next time.

Praise: If students are giving speeches, invite everyone to record, during each presentation, what the presenter does well. As the presenter concludes, invite the class to offer verbal praise about the strengths of the presentation. Highlighting strengths and sharing these verbally is not only inspiring and motivating, it also helps other learners know how to do the same thing.

HINT:

You might not get every class or presentation to go perfectly, but even in difficulty, you can find a location where things are going well. Pay attention to what is working and spend time working to increase that success rate.

Visualize: It is important that your learners are also thinking about the best of the best. Before an event, have your students visualize what success would look like, and then have them record their ideas and share them with each other. They will come up with amazing ideas! For example, if you are having groups working together, have all learners individually write about what it takes for groups to work well together. Once they write their ideas, have them share with partners and then with the entire group. The entire group can take notes on all the great ideas and your learners will be visualizing what success will look like.

34. Create a circle

In many communities, gathering people into a circle is an important event. It is important because it includes everyone, connects everyone and supports everyone in being with each other in real ways. In a banking model of education, the intention of learning is about filling individuals with facts. In a model designed to unleash learning, connection, collaboration and communication are essential. Not only that, something powerful happens when you sit in a circle of your peers.

Creating a circle is also a great strategy for "riding the wave". For instance, if energy drops in your session you can ask everyone to stand and move into a circle. The key, though, is to ensure you have set up the learning space during your preparation process to allow for this to happen.

TIPS FOR WORKING IN A CIRCLE

1. When standing or sitting, ensure everyone is connected. Ensure chairs are close to each other or, if standing, ensure everyone is standing almost shoulder-to-shoulder.

2. Ensure learners are not sitting behind desks.

3. Assign everyone a partner to work with in the circle. Ideally partners are sitting next to each other. Partners are a great way for people to share together before speaking to the larger group.

4. Before inviting individuals to speak to the group in the circle, provide time for individuals to speak first with their partners. This helps lower the filter, helps learners think through their ideas and ensures everyone is lifting the weights, even if they choose not to share in the full group.

5. Be in a circle, but don't go in a circle. That is to say, invite individuals to share when they are ready to share. If you ask individuals to speak from one person to the next around the circle, learners will not fully pay attention. They will be thinking with some fear of what they will say when it is their turn. And once they have shared, with relief, may not fully pay attention to the next person. Allowing individuals to share when ready is a great way to lower the filter and support everyone lifting the weights.

6. If standing in a circle, invite individuals to sit down after they have shared. Because you are using a circle, rather than going in a circle, it's a great way to encourage everyone to share.

7. A circle is a great way to create a powerful closing.

35. Circle back

Sometimes learning can be like putting students on a train—it can feel like the only goal is to get to all the stops and reach the final destination within a specific timeframe. Unfortunately, with this approach, it can be easy for learners to forget where they have been and simply focus on reaching the destination. At the end, they might remember a few of the stops, but over time, might forget they took the ride all together.

To unleash learning, it is essential that you circle back. Rather than explore one concept or idea once and move on to the next stop, it is important those "stops" are reviewed often.

When I raise the idea of circling back, you might say "I only have so much time, and we have a lot of information to get through!" This might be true, but if you want learning to be unleashed for *everyone*, it is essential that all learners lift weights on concepts, ideas and new knowledge over and over again.

I am not talking about reteaching. Rather, I suggest that in a one-hour class, a three-hour workshop, or full-week retreat, there will be a lot of learning taking place, and by circling back and lifting the weights once again, you are ensuring that all learners will keep this important work with them for a very long time.

> # HINT:
>
> Circling back is a reminder to find ways for your learners to review the main ideas, experiences, concepts or topics you believe are essential, and find quick strategies to get them to lift the weights on these again and again. Rather than having your session be a train that only goes forward, circling back is a reminder that for learning to be unleashed, we all need to lift the weights over and over again!

SIMPLE WAYS TO CIRCLE BACK

1. At the start of a session, put a few questions on the PowerPoint slide that relate directly to the topics, ideas or events that were covered during the previous session. After you have your students write first on one of the questions, ask everyone to stand up and answer the questions with their partners.

2. If you are giving a talk or running a session that has a break built into it, circle back when everyone returns from the break. You can have a few specific questions on PowerPoint and have partners answer the questions together.

3. Have a few specific topics, questions or ideas that you will want your learners to revisit. These questions might focus on the main ideas that have been previously covered These items are the weights you want your learners to consistently lift.

HOW TO END

》》 The ending of a session is a critical time for the learning process. It's the time for all learners to make meaning of the session and, hopefully, leave your learners wanting more. Here are two sure-fire ways to ensure that learning is fully unleashed in a strategic and mindful way.

PART II

>> HOW TO END

36. Always write last

One way that learning is unleashed is in the moment when one has to make sense of an experience for oneself. That is, a person can watch a movie, sit through a talk, read a book, or be in a class, but learning is not fully unleashed until he or she explains the movie, book, talk or lesson in his or her own words. Just like a weightlifter must lift weights to build muscle, one of the best ways to ensure everyone is lifting the weights is to get learners to write. When the pen or pencil is hitting the page, you can be more confident that learning is being unleashed for your students. Through writing, students have an opportunity to think through their own thoughts, opinions and ideas. Writing is a great way to both start off a class and to finish a class.

Think of it this way. Have you ever read a few pages of a book, and didn't realize you didn't fully understand what it was about until you had to talk about it with someone else? Or maybe you watched a movie, and it wasn't until someone asked you to explain it that you had to really think through what the movie was about?

HINT:

The end of a learning session is a critical time to unleash learning. By creating an opportunity for your learners to strategically write last, you are providing an opportunity for *all* learners to make meaning for the session they just experienced. This will help unleash their learning.

>> HOW TO GET EVERYONE TO WRITE LAST

- Ask everyone to write 30 words or less on what the session was about for them. When people are done, have them share their responses with their partner, and ask a few people to then share their responses (limit it to three) to the entire group.

- Show the agenda, and provide two minutes for everyone to record how they would describe what the session was about to someone who wasn't in the room. Again, have them share with their partner, and have a few share with the full group.

- Provide sentence starters (I think, I feel, I'm curious) and ask everyone to complete a few sentences and then share them with partners, and then the full group.

37. Create powerful closings

You have set your learners up for success. You had them write first, speak with their partners and lift the weights throughout the learning session. You put an agenda on the board and you checked for understanding throughout the session. How do you capture the success of the session that both highlights everyone's learning and leaves everyone wanting more? Create a powerful closing.

Creating a powerful closing helps learners make meaning of your session. It might leave them feeling inspired to leave your class wanting to make a difference. It might cause them to think deeply about the main topic of your presentation. It might help create a sense of closure, especially if they took your session over an extended period of time.

If you are serious and committed to unleashing learning for everyone (I know you are), the way you end the session matters! If you are teaching a class session or giving a presentation, you might spend just a few minutes on the closing of the session. If you have had a group for an extended period of time, you might devote the last full session to your closing.

> **HINT:**
>
> However you create a powerful closing, don't forget that the meaning and learning will be unleashed by getting everyone to lift the weights. What is important is not just what you do for the closing, but ensuring that it is created in a way that unleashes learning for all. When your learners speak it, write it, summarize it, discuss it, read it or explain it, they are lifting the weights. To create the kind of closing that unleashes learning for everyone, ensure everyone is fully lifting the weights as you close *together*.

Remember, you just created an important learning experience, and the wisdom, wonder, excitement and meaning of that session will be brought to the next level by ensuring you create a powerful closing.

CREATE A POWERFUL CLOSING

- Use a poem, story or quote that connects to the class or presentation and helps inspire everyone. Have partners, or the entire group, read the text out loud.

- Have the group sit in a circle as part of the closing.

- Ask partners who have been working together throughout the session to shake hands and thank each other.

- Provide time for everyone to write last on the main ideas they have learned. Provide time for groups to share with each other what they wrote.

- Have them read out loud the summaries of their notes, main learning, or use sentence starters (such as "I think…", "I feel…", "I'm learning…").

- Play music for the group as they are leaving.

- Shake everyone's hands at the end of the session.

There is wisdom to be harvested at the end of a learning session. The way you consider the work that took place, the aspects of the session that worked well and those aspects that didn't, are critical to the success you continue to create. It can be tempting to finish a class session and quickly move on to the next task. Yet, to unleash learning for everyone, it is important that you critically reflect on the session. Sometimes a section of the learning session might not go well, and you beat yourself up for it. Or you can think through that area that didn't go well and make changes for next time. There are many ways to reflect on your practice, and in the following pages, I offer a few areas to consider as part of your reflection.

PART III
>> REFLECT

38. Change the rules of the game

I once met a teacher who told me she never attended lectures when she went to university. When I asked why, she simply said, "They didn't require it." While she was very motivated to get through university, she also understood the rules of the game and played accordingly. That meant she went to very few classes.

When I was teaching at the university, many students told me they never read any of the textbooks. When I asked them why, they told me that most of the teachers assigned the readings, but never mentioned them or used the readings in their classes, so they didn't see reading as important.

The learners we work with know the rules of our game and are playing these rules well. Sometimes these rules are made explicit (you must be here on time; you lose points for late assignments; put phones away before we begin), but more often there are hidden rules, which students figure out quickly, and play accordingly.

Here are some examples:

Situation: Students don't turn in assignments consistently.

Hidden Rule: The teacher doesn't give points for all assignments, so I know I don't have to do everything.

Situation: Students don't bring supplies.

Hidden Rule: If I don't bring my things, I usually don't have to do much that day.

Situation: Participants text or talk to people during sessions.

Hidden Rule: It's okay because I have really important things going on and I'm not being that rude.

Situation: Two students walk into your session very late, holding coffees they just purchased. They disrupt the group as they try to catch up with what they have missed.

Hidden Rule: There are no consequences for being late, so we can come when we see fit.

If you find yourself in these situations, you can tell stories about your learners (they aren't very motivated, and so on), get upset about what you see going on, or chastise the entire group for these behaviors. Nothing is worse than having to address these things with learners, either as a group or individually. Such reactive conversations rarely go well, and often break the community of trust you have worked hard to establish. Rather than react, become an astute observer that sees these situations as a gift that highlights the rules of the game! These hidden rules are often the reasons why learning is not fully unleashed for *everyone*.

Once you can see the rules, you can mindfully, creatively, carefully, kindly, proactively and courageously change the rules of the game, rules that create stronger systems that unleash learning for everyone! Simply put,

it's hard to get learning unleashed if individuals are talking, texting, coming to the session late, sitting with their friends, not bringing supplies or not turning in work. You can change this game, but you have to create proactive systems that eliminate the patterns that limit success for you and all your learners.

HINT:

Often learning is not unleashed for *everyone* because there are systemic rules that are in place. Changing the rules of the game can bring out the best in you and all your learners!

CREATING NEW RULES

Situation: In the past participants have come late to sessions.

New Rule: At the start of your first session, provide time for teams to come up with a list of values related to participation. Make sure arriving to the session on time makes the lists. Have everyone agree to these guidelines and revisit them often. At the start of each session, thank everyone for being on time, and ensure you actually start on time.

Situation: You give a talk and everyone is sitting in the back of the room, which makes it very difficult to interact with the group. You find yourself asking people to move closer, but few are willing to.

New Rule: Get to the venue early, and place yellow pieces of paper on where you would like people to sit. Put up a PowerPoint slide with "Please collect your inspiration by sitting where there is a yellow piece of paper." On the pieces of paper are inspiring quotes that connect to your talk. Stand by the front door and shake people's hands as they enter and ask them to sit where the paper is. Without being reactive, you have a group sitting in the perfect location where learning can be unleashed—and they didn't even need to know what, how or why you did what you did. You rock!

YOU

39. Shine the light on you

Imagine you are holding a flashlight in a darkened room. You can point the flashlight in only two directions. One is away from you, so that when you move the flashlight around, it shines light into different parts of the room. The other is pointed towards you. Depending on where you point the flashlight, your legs, feet, torso or head are filled with light. In this direction, the flashlight is lighting you up.

If you are reading this book, you are probably in a giving profession in which the task at hand is to give, lead, teach, serve, help out or be of assistance in some capacity. In these activities, the flashlight is always pointed away from you. And every time you go for professional development, sit through meetings, listen to a talk or read a professional journal, I'm guessing most of that time is focused on items that continue to point the flashlight out into the darkened room. In this professional arena, it can be hard to be reminded to point the light at yourself! But that is exactly what I am reminding you to do.

You can memorize the strategies of this book, be confident about the materials you are using and be clear about the intentions of the work you are doing, but as we said at the start of this book, who you are matters. So I want to remind you to continually point the flashlight towards yourself.

Balance out the giving, teaching, serving, educating and leading for others, with giving, teaching, servicing, educating and leading for you. That's right, you! Your learners, audience, students or participants are engaging with *you*. And while the strategies, frameworks and skills in this book are critical to unleashing learning for everyone, so, too, is an educator who has a full, rich, healthy, balanced, congruent life.

I'm guessing that as you read this, you may already use these tools. But I'm also guessing that the biggest challenge for you is making time for many of these things as well. The best way I know to make this a reality is to put appropriate tools into your calendar. For instance, if you make the decision to get a monthly massage (you deserve it!), this will only really happen if you put it in your calendar. If your intention is to get more sleep, you might need to diarize the time you will be waking up each morning and going to bed at night. Your calendar is a great resource that, if used effectively, can support you in bringing out the best in your own life.

HINT:

Learn the strategies of this book. Work to find ways to support all of your learners to lift the weights. But, ultimately, your learners are engaging with you. The world needs your gifts and talents. To set them free, continue to shine the flashlight back on you!

SHINING THE LIGHT ON YOU

- Get a massage.
- Get therapy.
- Hire a coach.
- Work out.
- Attend a weekend retreat.
- Go watch live comedy.
- Call in sick when you are sick!
- Learn to say no!
- Leave work on time.
- Don't answer every email.
- Take a walk during lunch.
- Eat lunch outdoors.
- Schedule a physical.
- Read inspirational poetry.
- Get more sleep.
- Accept praise.
- Maintain healthy boundaries.
- Create a life you love.
- Give up the need to please.
- Let go of perfectionism.
- Face your fears.
- Be daring.
- Be bold.
- Make yourself proud.
- Cook healthy meals.
- Be around inspiring people.

40. Use technology but don't be used by it

Let's imagine you are standing on one side of a very wide river, and your goal is to get to the other side. The currents are too strong for you to swim, but fortunately you are being provided with items that can assist you. Your intention is to get to the other side, so you only select the tools that will serve this purpose. While there are many tools to choose from, you decide to use a canoe, life jacket and an oar. You get into the boat, and with these tools, you row to the other side.

Keep this story in mind when you are using technology to unleash learning. Why? Because you now have a vast array of technology tools at your disposal, and you can either use these in the service of your intentions, or you can be used by them and find they are actually undermining, distracting or limiting (yes,

limiting) your ability to create the conditions that will unleash learning for *all*. As an educator, the technology you have at your disposal is simply astonishing. With mindful, thoughtful, clearly defined intentions, you can use these tools to unleash learning for everyone (yes, everyone). Without mindfulness, you may find yourself trying to get to the other side of the river, but not getting anywhere at all.

Let me give you an example:

Example 1: Your intentions are to activate prior knowledge, build community and lower the filter to unleash learning for everyone. You see that sometimes students need more time to feel safe enough to share their ideas, and you believe that providing time for learners to get to know each other and exchange ideas is an important tool to unleash learning for all. With these intentions in mind, you find that using an online discussion forum where students log in, share their ideas to specific questions and talk with each other, will help with your intentions. Over time, you see that this tool is transforming your learning. Students are bringing the online discussions into the discussions that are taking place in your class session. You see the online forum as a way of gauging who is lifting the weights by the kinds of discussions that are taking place before you meet face-to-face. You see this tool as a resource for building community with important implications for the ways your learners engage with each other, think about the topics they are exploring, as well as helping provide more depth in your face-to-face sessions. This technology is dramatically supporting learning being unleashed for everyone!

Example 2: Your lectures can be recorded and made available to students online. You think this might be an amazing tool for your learners who have to miss class or want to review the session. You use this technology, but over time you start seeing that students are not coming to class—they can get the session online. You find your class sessions are now becoming smaller and smaller and, worse, your students are now just scanning the materials and not really engaging with the learning. You see that this technology tool is undermining your intention of building community and activating prior knowledge, and your ability to support learners lifting the weights. While students are able to pass assignments, you question how deep their learning is or how transformative these sessions can become, when they are simply scanning the materials.

HINT:

We are all being transformed by the wave of technology that is sweeping the world. It is changing our systems, our thinking, our ways of connecting. The speed at which it is taking place often offers little time to think through these technologies, their implications, and how they fit within frameworks, goals and our intentions. That is why it is essential that you mindfully use technology as an important tool to help you and your learners cross the river with success.

FINAL THOUGHTS. A MESSAGE TO YOU!

As you continue to work to unleash learning for everyone, I want to thank you for your courage. It takes courage to do the work you do. You might get funny looks when you try new things and work to ensure all your learners are lifting the weights. Your students, colleagues, participants, even staff might think you are not "teaching" them anything since they are writing, speaking, explaining, discussing, reading, questioning, or teaching each other like never before. But you know that learning is happening.

There will also be days when, despite the best planning, coordination and effort, the learning session falls apart or you or your learners are simply not at your best. During those times, you might feel vulnerable, doubtful or ready to give up. You might think your colleagues have this work all figured out, and you are the only one facing any challenges. But from my own experience, the times that don't go well can be a catalyst for finding ways to improve next time.

Please continue to be courageous. Our world needs your gifts, talents, insights and ways of knowing and being like never before. In addition, your work brings us together, helps us think in new ways, creates equity, helps improve our work or our lives, challenges us, inspires us and helps us all get better. My hope is that this book reminds you of your brilliance, and provides you with additional strategies to help that brilliance shine.

May you continue to shine!

ABOUT THE AUTHOR

Dr. William DeJean — Inspiration Unleashed

For over 20 years, Dr William DeJean (www.williamdejean.com) has inspired and re-inspired individuals and organizations for the important work they do. His work has helped thousands of people around the world reach their full potential.

Starting his career as a high school teacher, William inspired students to become the first in their families to attend university. For his successes, he received numerous recognitions, including being selected Teacher of the Year among 26,000 teachers in San Diego County.

William brings many lenses to the organizations he works with. He has taught at universities in the United States and Australia, he is an internationally recognized researcher, he consults across a range of social service and community organizations, and is a sought-after keynote speaker, including appearances at TEDx Canberra and the Young Minds Conference.

He can be reached at **william@williamdejean.com**

CPSIA information can be obtained
at www.ICGtesting.com
Printed in the USA
FSOW03n1004110516
20316FS